Golf on the Tundra

The Official Rulebook of the Tundra Golf Association

BAD DOG PRESS™

Bad Dog Press
P.O. Box 130066
Roseville, MN 55113

World WideWeb: http://www.octane.com

Golf on the Tundra: The Official Rule Book of the Tundra Golf Association

First published in 1996

Printed in the United States of America.
96 97 98 99 00   10 9 8 7 6 5 4 3 2 1

Text: Tony Dierckins, Tim Nyberg, and The Frozen Foursome: Jim "Ice" Berg, Tony "Dr. Storm" Smith, Paul Whitelaw "Winter Rules" Gorski, and Ron "Frozen Bear" Stierman

Illustrations/Photography: Tim Nyberg and Paul Gorski

ISBN 1-887317-09-0
Library of Congress Catalog Card Number: 96-084850

Warning: Contains humor, a highly volatile substance if used improperly. Harmful if swallowed. All content is a fictional product of the authors' imaginations. Any resemblance between characters portrayed herein and actual persons living, dead, or residing in New Jersey is purely coincidental. Contents under pressure. Do not use near open flame. Do not use as a flotation device, or at least avoid any situations in which you would need to rely on a book as a flotation device. Any typographic errors are purely intentional and left for your amusement. Always say no to drugs and, by all means, stay in school.

For all golfers who welcome winter as the
beginning of the tundra golf season
rather than the end of their year on the
course—those brave linksters who
never consider storing their clubs.

The Frozen Foursome thanks
Door County's Idlewild Golf Course
(located just north of the frozen tundra of
the Green Bay Packers' Lambeau Field)
for allowing us to pursue our addiction.
You were aware of our winter games,
weren't you?

And a special thanks to our wives, for always
saying "Have a nice round, guys" instead of
"We hope you freeze, you sad little men!"

CONTENTS

INTRODUCTION

First of all, we'd like to point out that Tundra Golf is in no way associated with any winter golfing event that uses tennis balls. Tundra Golf is simply, as its name implies, golf played on a frozen, often snow-covered, course. Yet Tundra Golf is so much more than just golf played during the winter months. It is a game that requires dedication. It is a game that requires passion. Above all, it is a game that requires warm clothes.

Tundra Golf also requires an addiction to golf. Those who golf the tundra tend not only to *want* to play golf, but to *need* to play. No matter what else is going on in the tundra golfer's life, golf comes first. Marriage, children, religion, career, health—all play second fiddle to getting on the links for a round or two as far as the tundra golfer is concerned.

You probably received this book as a gift from someone who thinks you're addicted to golf. If you bought it yourself, you probably are addicted to golf. In either case, we're here to help.

continued ...

We're not suggesting you somehow overcome your "problem"—who are we to judge? If you are addicted to golf and, like us, can't afford to move to warmer climes, *Golf on the Tundra: the Official Rule Book of the T.G.A* provides you with a guide to facilitate ~~your addiction~~ winter play. Don't think of these "rules" as a set of hard and fast regulations. In fact, feel free to adapt our suggestions. The important thing is that you get out there and play and avoid the pain of withdrawal!

— The Frozen Foursome

*(Jim "Ice" Berg, Tony "Dr. Storm" Smith,
Paul Whitelaw "Winter Rules" Gorski,
and Ron "Frozen Bear" Stierman)*

PART 1

THE PLAY

❄ *Jim "Ice" Berg makes his way down the 14th fairway of the Lake Michigan Golf & Ice Fishing Club, Sturgeon Bay, Wisconsin.*

Basic Play

Tundra Golf is simply golf played between the first day of fall that the ground freezes and the first day of spring that thawing snow renders the course too wet and icky to walk on (basically, the time public courses "close" for the winter).

Like "traditional" golf, players hit a small, hard ball with specially designed clubs that consist of a wooden or metal club head attached to a metal shaft.*

There are, however, several other important distinctions between T.G.A. play and U.S.G.A. play. Read on!

*The safety of using graphite or other composite clubs in the extreme cold has not yet been established —none of the current members of the T.G.A. can afford such equipment, so these clubs remain untested in tundra extremes. Use at your own risk.

The Goal

In Tundra Golf, the goal is for players to hit the ball into the hole or "cup" (or its duly-sanctioned substitute; see **"Green" Play**) using as few strokes as possible and *without* freezing their extremities.

The Course

A standard tundra golf course is divided into eighteen holes that are, coincidentally, located on the same piece of real estate as most public golf courses sanctioned by the U.S.G.A.*

---

* *Players may establish their own courses on frozen rivers, lakes, or any open area as agreed upon by the players.*

BASIC EQUIPMENT

As many as fourteen different clubs may be used, depending on the length of shot required or the terrain, and each player may also carry up to three implements of snow removal such as a broom, a shovel, or a blow-torch.

❋ *The well-equipped winter golf cart often carries a fog-proof mirror to help check for frostbite.*

OBSTACLES

Typical obstacles found in U.S.G.A. play—such as water, tall grass called "rough," or traps filled with sand—are eliminated in tundra golf play: water is frozen, the rough is flattened with frost or covered in snow, and sand traps are often as hard as concrete, creating an opportunity for bounce and, therefore, greater distance on some shots.

Tundra Golf hazards include blowing and drifting snow, snow banks that swallow balls, frozen (extremely fast) greens, dangerously thin ice, and, occasionally, local authorities enforcing trespassing laws.

DETERMINING A WINNER

After eighteen holes, the winner of the round is the player with the lowest number of strokes, the fewest lost balls, and the highest overall body temperature. Winners of Tundra Golf tournaments are determined by identifying which player, after four rounds, either has the best (lowest) cumulative score or was the only player foolish enough to stay outside for four rounds.

 Winter or summer, sinking a difficult putt is always a thrill (7th "green" of The St. Nicholas Nine; North Pole, Polar Ice Cap).

ADVANTAGES OF TUNDRA GOLF

While it may seem that the only basic difference between U.S.G.A. golf and T.G.A. golf is that Tundra Golf is played when U.S.G.A. courses are closed due to snow and cold, there are several significant differences in the subtleties of the rules.

The T.G.A.'s Frozen Foursome believes that Tundra Golf has many, many advantages over its warm-weather cousin, including those listed on the following pages.

Tundra Golf Advantages:
Playing Conditions

- Many built-in excuses for playing poorly.

- Water hazards and sand traps actually helpful when frozen—bounce adds distance to your shots.

- If you loose track of strokes, you can backtrack in the snow for an accurate count.

- Leafless trees easier to see through.

- Continually drifting snow provides golf course with ever-changing contours and challenges.

- Fewer mosquitoes.

- Extreme cold's effect on ball compression makes 400-yard drives typical.

- Extra layers of clothes create a naturally slow, "Fred-Couples-like" tempo to your backswing.

- No "fried egg" lies in the sand traps.

Tundra Golf Advantages:
Less Peripheral Work

- Frozen sand traps never need raking.
- Blowing snow naturally replaces divots.
- Ski-hill towropes aid in uphill travel.
- Beverages stay cold; no need for a cooler!

Tundra Golf Advantages:
Lack of Other Golfers

- Guaranteed best parking spaces.
- No tee times needed.
- Play at your own pace.
- Free membership.

Tundra Golf Advantages:
Friendlier Atmosphere

- Earmuffs muffle your partners'/
  opponents' heckling remarks.

- Since the entire course is usually
  covered with snow, there are usually
  no hard feelings over evoking the
  "casual water" rule.

- Slow play eliminated by the need to
  stay warm—no cursing aimed at the
  foursome of hackers making you wait
  at each tee.

❄ *Careful! That winter sun can give you a nasty burn if you don't take proper precautions. (Mt. Everest Climbing, Rappelling, & Golf Club; Nepal)*

Tundra Golf's "Family Friendly Advantage Package"

Perhaps the greatest advantage to Tundra Golf is that it is a family-friendly activity. We're not suggesting that you take the kids out and expose them to the elements, but simply that certain conditions make golfing the tundra more "pro-family" than traditional golf—at least it does for those of us who make up the Frozen Foursome.

First, the limited daylight hours during winter months make Tundra Golf a weekend-only sport, ~~forcing us to spend more time~~ providing us with more time to spend with our wives and children.

Next, with clubhouses closed for the season, there is no bar or "19th Hole" to draw us into potentially inebriating activities.

And finally, the course itself is free of scantily dressed summertime "barmaids" motoring around on golf carts, using their feminine wiles, flirtatious smiles, and dreamy eyes to tempt us into purchasing malt-and-hop-based beverages.

This may sound sexist—that all winter golfers are men easily tempted by a cold beer and the fairer sex. ("Fairer sex." Now *that's* sexist.) Although we, the Frozen Foursome, are men, we don't think of ourselves as sexist. We simply haven't encountered any female tundra golfers. Our wives suggest that the reason for this may be that women golfers find something better to do with their time during winter months. Unfortunately, we can't imagine what that could possibly be.

The Disadvantages of Tundra Golf

- The limited daylight hours during the winter months make Tundra Golf a weekend-only sport.

- With clubhouses closed for the season, there is no bar or "19th Hole" to draw us into potentially inebriating activities.

- The course is free of scantily dressed summertime "barmaids" motoring around on golf carts, using their feminine wiles, flirtatious smiles, and dreamy eyes to tempt us into purchasing malt-and-hop-based beverages.

Tundra Golf is not a sport in which one should be concerned with fashion.

❄ **DRESS for SURVIVAL!** ❄

This has been a public service announcement brought to you by the Frozen Foursome.

PART 2

OFFICIAL "RULES" OF THE TUNDRA GOLF ASSOCIATION

❄ *Teeing off from a natural ice formation—just
one of the many flexible "rules" of T.G.A. play!
(Blizzard Valley Golf & Tennis; Donner's Pass,
Colorado)*

ABOUT THE "RULES"

The Tundra Golf Association suggests that first-time tundra golfers use the following "rules" as a guideline to getting started playing in the colder months.

As you become comfortable with winter play, feel free to adjust these guidelines as necessary to adapt play to courses in your region, eliminate whining among fellow players, and prevent colds and flu.

1. ATTIRE

Those who choose to participate in Tundra Golf should do so without worrying themselves over a matching ensemble. Instead, remember these three rules:

1. Layers

2. Layers

3. Layers

That's right—it doesn't matter what you look like, as long as you keep warm. With that in mind, you may also wish to consider the following advice:

1a. *Body Piercing*

> While the T.G.A. has no official position on self-mutilation, it does recommend removing all flesh-attached metal adornments from areas of the skin that will be exposed during play. Nothing conducts the cold quite like metal, so leaving that ring in your nose is just asking for frostbite.

1b. *Footware*

Snowmobile boots offer the best combination of warmth and a good solid base for a balanced swing. Boots may be adapted with chains or clip on spikes for traversing ice floes *(see the ad for TundraCo's Tundra-Taps™ below)*. Use of snowshoes or cross-country skis is not recommended (see **Trekking Restrictions**).

1c. *Gloves*

While many golfers use a golf glove to enhance their grip on the club, these lightweight hand coverings do little to protect from the cold. The T.G.A. recommends that you wear a mitten over the golf glove and remove it when shooting. Your non-gloved hand should also be mittened. Many Tundra Golfers develop their own system of degloving and regloving. The important thing is to keep your hands warm enough so you retain feeling— and a solid grip on the club!

 "Overgloving" is the practice of wearing a mitten over the golf glove. This important technique prevents frostbite and finger loss.

1d. *Hunting Season*

If you choose to do your Tundra Golfing during your state's or province's hunting season, remember to wear lots of blaze orange or other bright, non-animal colors. Camouflage attire, though generally quite comfy, is not recommended, especially if you are playing on a course close to wooded areas or lakes and farm fields that provide habitat to deer, moose, elk, and game fowl.

We also recommend that players avoid wearing novelty headware inspired by Bullwinkle J. Moose.

1e. *Plaid*

In light of the recent trendiness of plaid, the T.G.A. feels compelled to clarify its position. Since the T.G.A. is dedicated to the abolition of styles worn in response to popular music rather than practicality or a reflection of heritage, it restricts the use of plaids to Tundra Golfers (and alternative musicians) of Scottish descent and those who hail from Canada or U.S. states *west* of Lake Michigan and *above* the 45th parallel: Alaska, Oregon, Washington, Idaho, Montana, the Dakotas, Minnesota, Wisconsin, and Michigan's Upper Peninsula. Vermont *natives* may also wear plaid.

Exceptions: The T.G.A. does, however, recognize that many plaids are printed on flannel material, an essential element of any Tundra Golf ensemble. Because of this, players who do not fit the restrictions may wear flannel plaids while Tundra Golfing but will be assessed a two-stroke penalty if discovered wearing a non-flannel plaid or any plaid at an alternative music club.

❄ *Ron "Frozen Bear" Stierman modeling his choice of Tundra Golf apparel. (Frostbite Falls Snowmobile & Golf Club; International Falls, Minnesota)*

2. THE BALL

The ball a player uses shall conform to the same restrictions as those specified by the U.S.G.A. However, the T.G.A. highly recommends that players use colored balls. The use of white balls usually results in extremely slow play as players try to locate balls in the backdrop of snow. Extended exposure to the elements while searching for a ball can cause frostbite or even hypothermia, which in turn often results in discomfort, death, or, sadly, poor play.

2a. *Lost Balls*

If a player loses a ball, he or she may drop another ball where the original ball was last sighted—without penalty! Remember: a lost ball is not worth death by exposure.

2c. *Lack of Balls*

If a player loses or destroys all the balls in his bag, that player may purchase a ball from his or her partner in order to continue play. The player choosing this option does so with the penalty of one stroke and the risk that fellow Tundra Golfers may joke that the player "has no balls."

2d. *Heated Balls*

TundraCo has recently developed the HeaterBall,™ a battery-powered golf ball that melts surrounding snow to assure a great lie *(see ad on page 28)*. While not currently sanctioned, the ball is under consideration. Players must decide prior to a match if they wish to allow the use of heated balls (easily amused readers may add their own joke here).

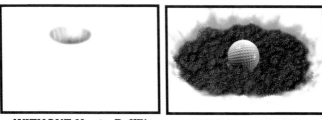

3. CADDIES

Golfers playing under T.G.A. rules are allowed one caddie to carry a player's bag and snow removal implements and/or transport the player throughout the course.

Caddies are rare since convincing someone to carry your stuff and tote you around outdoors in subfreezing temperatures takes considerable negotiation skills.

Because of this, any player using a *willing* caddie (one who does *not* owe the player money or is *not* currently being blackmailed by the player) may deduct two strokes from his or her final score *if* the caddie remains in service for the entire match.

4. CASUAL WATER

Casual water, according to the U.S.G.A., is "any temporary accumulation of water on the course which is visible before or after the player takes his stance and is not in a water hazard. Snow and natural ice, other than frost, are casual water.…" It also allows for relief: a player can improve his lie from casual water so long as the ball is not moved closer to the cup.

The T.G.A. follows this same rule, but does so with the understanding that when playing Tundra Golf, the entire course is one great big mass of casual water! Therefore, players may seek relief before *each* shot!

Players should note, however, that they may not invoke the casual water rule if their ball lands on a frozen water hazard, such as a lake, pond, or stream. Since these hazards would have swallowed a ball during summer play, the T.G.A. considers it advantage enough that a player can even locate and address his or her ball. Taking relief would be making a mockery of the game.

5. EQUIPMENT

During T.G.A. play a golfer must adhere to the same fourteen-club rule as outlined in U.S.G.A. rules. However, the T.G.A. allows for snow-removal implements (see **Snow**) as well as certain equipment modifications as outlined on the following pages.

5a. *Club Modifications*

For safety and improved play, the T.G.A. allows for some club modifications. All modified equipment presented in this book that includes a ™ is a trademarked product of TundraCo, the unofficial manufacturer of the T.G.A. and sponsor of *Golf On the Tundra*. Look for their ads throughout this book.

• The StudClub™

A club, either a wood or an iron, whose head is equipped with studs to reduce or eliminate bounce: when you hit the solid tundra with an object as lethal as a golf club, you want as little bounce as possible.

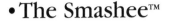

• The Smashee™

A club, usually an iron, equipped with a metal spike that digs under the ice and snow to improve a player's lie just before the club face strikes the ball.

• The Frozen Spoon™

A club, either a wood or an iron, equipped with a shovel or "spoon" device that, on a player's backswing, removes snow so that the club's follow-through is unabated.

• Maximum shaft flex

The T.G.A. has no restrictions on shaft flex. In fact, most Tundra Golfers will laugh at you if you bring it up: In this weather, it's almost impossible for a shaft not to be stiff.

(By all means, insert your own joke here.)

❄ *Ron "Frozen Bear" Stierman demonstrates the improper way to test shaft flex.*

5b. *Non-Club Modifications*

• Metal-alloy tees

While Tundra Golf players are encouraged to tee off from nontraditional surfaces (see **Teeing Off**), those who wish may use traditional tees. However, since ground is frozen during T.G.A. play, normal wooden tees often break. Tees made of metal easily p e n e t r a t e most terrain.

❄ *Teeing from a mound of hand-piled snow. (Moose Jaw Cross Country Ski & Tundra Golf Resort, Moose Jaw, Saskatchewan, Canada)*

• Hammer

We recommend using a standard claw hammer for pounding tees into the ground (removing optional).

• Teeminator™

(see ad on right)

A gun-like device that drives metal-alloy tees into the frozen ground. Perfect for golfers who fear striking their thumbs with a hammer.

• Ice pick

Any ice pick available in hardware stores may be added to the bag for use in removing balls that have become lodged in ice walls.

• Ball warmer

Maintaining ball temperature is very important *(see pages 79-80)*. Try keeping your extra balls in a pair of battery-powered hunting socks.

• HotWash™ *(see ad below)*

A personal-size heated ball washer that cleans your ball and renders it free of ice. It also comes in handy as a source of hot water to help free golfers who have accidentally frozen their tongue to their putter-shaft while celebrating a birdied hole.

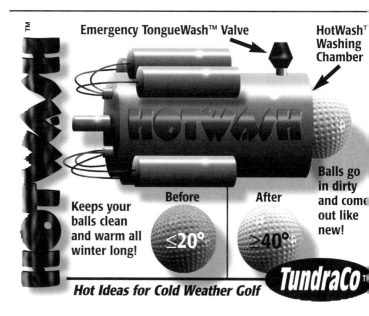

• Toddy-Pro™

Tundra Golfers can forget about carrying a cooler—the outside air guarantees you'll always have a cold one. However, beer freezes, and cans may explode if it gets cold enough. The Toddy-Pro™ protects golfers: This convenient beverage warmer keeps all beverages safely above freezing so you can enjoy a drink without fear of frozen lungs or exploding cans.

The folks at Toddy-Pro Inc. were undergoing financial "reorganization" when we were selling ads, but we decided to picture their product anyway.

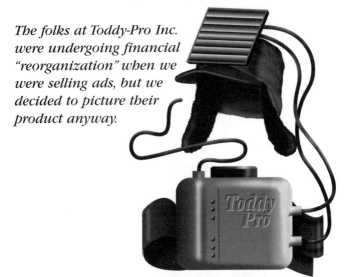

6. GREEN PLAY

To avoid misinterpretation of overlapping U.S.G.A. rules, the T.G.A. calls greens "greens" even though during T.G.A. play the greens are usually a mottled green and brown (depending on how much frost damage has occurred).

The greens may also be white if covered with snow, but the T.G.A. does not use "whites" in order to avoid confusion with discussions or recipes involving eggs.

Stick with standard U.S.G.A. rules except where they involve **Casual Water** or any of the circumstances on the following pages.

6a. *Flags*

Since most T.G.A. play occurs when a course is actually closed or on an area not regularly used for golf, players may mark holes with their own flags, sticks, or small children or pets—whatever is most convenient and can be seen from a distance.

If you are unable to remove a cup marker because it has become frozen, any ball touching the marker is considered in the hole. However, should the ball break the marker, the shot is deemed "too hard" and the ball is not considered in the hole.

If players are using a living marker and it becomes frozen or broken, T.G.A. etiquette calls for the immediate repair or resuscitation of said marker.

6b. *Snow-covered Greens*

Greens completely covered with snow or with enough to make snow removal a time-consuming pain in the posterior are automatic "two-putt" greens: Once you land on snow-covered green, add two strokes to those it took you to reach the green, record the total as your score for the hole, and move on to the next tee.

On partially covered greens, players may choose to move obstructed balls to another part of the green *no closer than the ball's original location* and finish the hole from there without penalty.

6c. *Clogged Cups*

If the ball touches any part of a hole filled with ice and/or snow, it's good! Clogged cups should be monitored by a partner. Any protests by opponents may be resolved with a blowtorch. If, however, opponents continue to protest, try melting the ice and snow in the hole.

6d. *Missing Cups*

If you cannot find the cup on the green, a glove or mitten may be used as a substitute. The hand covering should be thrown to a neutral position at least ten feet from the closest ball to avoid creating footprints in fresh powder. Players may not use a novelty "We're #1!" foam glove as a substitute cup *unless* they wear it while playing the entire round.

6e. *Ego Cups*

If a foursome is not having a good round, a jacket may be used as a substitute cup. This method is strictly used as an ego boost and should be employed on a very limited basis so as not to distract from the purity of the game and so that jacketless players may avoid prolonged exposure to the elements.

❄ *"Ego cup" utilized by the Frozen Foursome on a particularily bad day at the Coldwater Country Club, Tok, Alaska.*

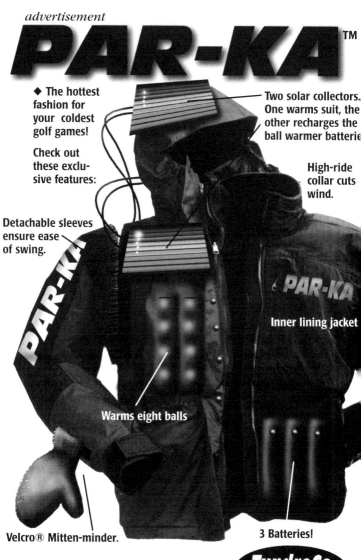

7. HANDICAPPING

Tundra Golf does not allow for traditional handicaps—playing in the winter is generally handicap enough to equalize scores among players of varying talents.

If players find a need to balance skill levels, handicapping is not assessed by eliminating strokes from the scores of lesser players, but by altering the ability of—literally *handicapping*—the better players. Choose from among the options on the ensuing pages.

7a. *Inappropriate Attire*

More skilled players are forced to play in warm-weather clothes, thus creating a chill whose resulting "shakes" are usually enough to force poor strokes.

7b. *Restricted Club Use*

More skilled players are forced to play with a limited number of clubs and without the modifications or snow removal implements allowed (see **Equipment** and **Snow**).

7c. *Increased Green Difficulty*

The opposite of allowing "Ego cups" (see rule 6e), players may handicap more skilled opponents by choosing the placement of the cup *after* the better player's ball has landed on the green. The less skilled players may also choose an unusually small glove or mitten to serve as a cup substitute.

7d. *Invoked Cliché*

More skilled players may have one hand tied behind their back or their eyes obstructed (the T.G.A. recommends some sort of blindfold to cover the eye as actual poking-out may interfere with future rounds when skills may be equal; it also helps avoid inconvenient personal injury litigation and complicated explanations on dismemberment insurance claims).

7e. *Exemption from T.G.A. Advantages*

Less skilled players can choose from among the official T.G.A. rules and render more skilled players exempt from its advantages. For example, handicapped players may be restricted from improving their lie as allowed herein.

8. HAZARDS

While traditional golf hazards are practically eliminated from Tundra Golf (roughs are snow-covered, water and sand frozen), the game does include some unique hazards not found during summer play. Keep the guidelines on the following pages in mind if you encounter those particular obstacles.

❄ *Care should be taken when dislodging balls from icy crevices. There is always the danger of starting an avalanche or being impaled by falling icicles. Wear protective gear!*

8a. *Sledders in the Fairway*

If a player's ball is interfered with by the head or body of a sledder, the player is allowed a drop where the ball *would* have landed or a free shot from the ball's original position.

8b. *Cross-country Skiers/Tracks*

Should a skier interfere with a player's backswing, the player is allowed to hit again without penalty. Cross-country ski and snowmobile tracks may be treated as you treat cart paths during the summer—free swing and stance relief.

8c. *Freezing on the Green*

This hazard is common among players who take too much time lining up their putts and is another good reason to avoid slow play, and can sometimes result in a penalty (see **Hypothermia**).

8d. *Snowmobiles*

While their tracks provide a great lie, snowmobiles themselves pose a great danger, as many drivers may not even see you as they scout the horizon for cross-country skiers to run over.

8e. *Irate Greenskeepers*

Unenlightened greenskeepers may not recognize the assets of Tundra Golf, under the misconception that play during winter months may damage a course. The truth is, the frozen ground actually protects turf from divotting.

However, should an angry groundsperson disrupt your round, play may be continued at a later date from the last hole finished with no penalty to any players.

9. HYPOTHERMIA

Hypothermia is such a dangerous hazard that T.G.A. officials have deemed it necessary to give it its own section in this book. Remember, Tundra Golf is a pro-family sport, and nothing breaks up a family faster than having one of its members freeze to death trying to get in a round of golf. We frown on this type of behavior.

Succumbing to the elements is the fault of ill-prepared or reckless tundra golfers, those who did not prepare themselves for the conditions or continued to play when it was too darn cold even for scramble play. Perhaps their play was so slow, they simply froze.

This, of course, creates dangers for fellow tundra golfers, who must brave the conditions to retrieve and revive hypothermia victims. Because of this, after reviving partner from slow-play hypothermia, players are allowed to assess their frozen colleague a two-stroke penalty.

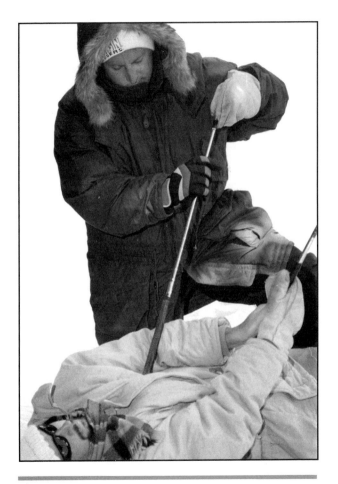

❄ *Reviving a hypothermic colleague—a two-stroke penalty for the victim! (Fifth hole, Mt. Everest Climbing, Rapelling, & Golf Club, Nepal)*

10. Limited Visibility

Blowing snow that reduces visibility is an inevitable aspect of almost any round of Tundra Golf. If, however, limited visibility creates extensive difficulty locating balls, players should consider the **Hypothermia** rule (#9). Players should use their best judgment and reach a consensus on whether to continue play.

11. Slow Play

Although slow play is seldom a concern during Tundra Golf, the T.G.A. frowns upon it for safety reasons. There usually aren't enough golfers on the course for slow play to disrupt a round, but those who play particularly slowly open themselves to the threat of hypothermia. If your party encounters a slow foursome, keep moving to avoid catching a chill. We recommend the activities on the following pages while you bide your time at the tee box.

❄ *Tony "Dr. Storm" Smith uses an ice auger during slow play to drill for lost balls in frozen water hazards. (Idlewild Golf Course; Door County, Wisconsin)*

• *Locate lost balls*

Borrow an ice auger from local ice anglers and look for balls in water hazards.

• *Create sculpture*

Bring along a chain saw and create an ice sculpture while you wait. Better yet, carry a welding torch so you can bide your time by reworking frustration-damaged clubs into a set for the kids—the heat from the torch will help keep you and your partners from freezing.

• *Attempt to build a fire*

Dust off your scouting skills and reenact Jack London stories at the same time you keep your fellow golfers warm and safe from slow-play hypothermia.

• *Build an igloo*

What better way to bide your time than to construct a windproof shelter right there on the links? Try to find a spot near several holes so you have a convenient retreat you can access throughout the round.

• *Practice your tracking skills*

Nothing leaves a clearer trail of animal movement than the snow. Turn downtime into another opportunity to be aggressively competitive—find out who among your foursome can identify the prints of the most woodland creatures. Extra points for live trapping!

12. SNOW

The Inuit People (or "Eskimos") have over 200 names for snow. While we recognize that snow comes in several varieties, we also recognize that having 200 different names for something is not only overkill but a clear sign that these people either have way too much time on their hands or live without the miracle of cable television.

Of course, the same could be said about those who choose to golf in subfreezing weather.

Whatever the case, the T.G.A. recognizes five varieties of snow, as listed in the chart on the right.

12a. *Official T.G.A. Snow Types*

HARD	Sometimes known as "ice," hard snow is, except for green play, ideal for Tundra Golf. Its surface usually allows players to walk with little difficulty, and bounces off its frozen surface often help add yardage to fairway shots. It also tends to leave clear holes where a ball enters a snow bank, allowing players to more easily finds their balls. On greens, however, it causes excessive roll and can cause a great deal of frustration. Casual Water rules apply.
SOFT	Called "fluffy" in some circles, soft snow can create difficulties because its lack of resistance can sometimes hide ball entry marks. It is, however, the easiest snow to remove, so players can improve their lies when invoking Winter Rules. Casual Water rules apply.
ICKY	Also called "slushy," icky snow is a combination of wet snow and ice about the same consistency as a 7-11 Slurpee,™ although its flavor choices are much more limited. It causes messy follow-throughs and requires players to wear waterproof boots. Casual Water rules apply.
BLOWING	Often simply soft or fluffy snow caught in the wind, blowing snow greatly reduces visibility, creating another good argument for the use of colored balls. Sometimes called a "blizzard." Ignore casual water or winter rules and follow the safety instructions of your local TV meteorologist.
YELLOW	Considered more of a hazard than a snow type, yellow snow is any of the above-described snow types tainted by the excess kidney-filtered bodily fluids of various animals, usually those of the canine variety. Players may seek relief by redropping the ball. Often, however, players choose to simply take a fresh ball from their bag and play on, particularly if the snow is also steaming.

12b. *Snowballing*

Snowballing is the phenomenon of a ball gathering snow as it rolls on a green or fairway, increasing the diameter of the ball with newly attached snow as it goes. If a "snowballed" ball lands on top of or next to the cup but is prevented from entering because of its increased size, a blowtorch may be used to remove the excess snow. If the ball settles into the hole, it counts. If no blowtorch is available, measure the circumference of the snowballed ball. If it is the same as or greater than the distance from the ball to the cup, the ball is considered "in" (see the formula below). This rule defies the traditional U.S.G.A. proverb "Never up, never in" and creates a new one for the T.G.A.: "Close enough for Tundra Golf."

$$\text{If } C \geq d,\ s = !$$

C = circumference of snow-covered ball;
d = distance from ball to center of cup;
s = shot; ! = Wee-hee!

12c. *Snow Redistribution*

Sweeping and shoveling greens, fairways, and roughs is allowed, and players are allowed a free drop when snow redistribution is complete (the player is therefore rewarded for his or her hard work, and for improving the playing conditions of those further back on the course). Some restrictions, however, do apply. Check the following pages.

• Additional equipment

Players may carry up to three snow removal implements (broom, shovel, blowtorch, etc.) in their bag. These do not count as part of the fourteen club rule (see *Basic Equipment* in **Part 1**). Players who wish to carry a fourth snow removal device may do so only after forfeiting a club of their choice.

• Snowblowers

Rulings on snowblowers tend to fall into a gray area. Generally, if a snowblower is attached to a vehicle being used as transportation by the players, or if it fits into a player's bag, it is allowed as part of Tundra Golf play. But for goodness sake, keep your hands out of that auger!

❄ *Powdery snow may be brushed from the putting path with a whisk broom. Note: players may legally carry three snow removal implements.*

• Out of bounds

You may not remove snow if attempting to play a ball out of bounds. Out of bounds is still out of bounds, even if the snow cover prevents you from determining what is out of bounds.

13. SUSPENDED PLAY

Players, upon a majority consensus, may suspend play because of limited visibility, wind-chill factor, lack of playable balls, encroaching dinnertime, or the sudden appearance of local law enforcement officers.

If play is suspended, it must be resumed at the next convenient opportunity at the tee of the unfinished hole. Unless, of course, the score-keeper loses the scorecard or is incarcerated for trespassing.

14. Teeing Off

Since tee boxes may be covered in snow and are almost always frozen solid, it is extremely difficult to implant traditional wooden tees while playing Tundra Golf.* Therefore, players may tee off under the conditions that follow.

Metal-alloy tees are available for those purists who feel they need a traditional tee.

14a. *Teeing "Off the Land"*

Like a camper "living off the land," using things found in nature, true Tundra Golfers choose to tee off from clumps of ice or snow they have shaped by hand to support their ball.

14b. *Substitute Tee Boxes*

Portable, substitute teeing ground used primarily when snow conditions render finding actual teeing grounds extremely difficult may be used if all players agree. These surrogate tee boxes can be covered in turf to duplicate traditional U.S.G.A. play or snow-covered for a fun, hearty T.G.A. round. Portable models such as TundraCo's Wintee™ *(see ad on opposite page)* come equipped with sled runners on their bases to help them move through snow. The player with the highest score on the previous hole is usually forced to bring the portable tee box to the next tee.

14c. *Ball Falling Off Tee*

Should a ball fall off a tee or snow clump before a player strikes it, it may be repositioned without penalty. If the ball continues to fall off due to wind, the scorekeeper should take temperature and wind speed readings and calculate the windchill. Windchills below -15°F are considered acceptable for suspension of play without penalty of being called "sissy-boy."

WINDCHILL INDEX FORMULA*

X = .303439 multiplied by sqr (wind speed) minus .0202886 multiplied by wind speed.

Windchill = (91.9 minus (91.4 minus degrees Fahrenheit) multiplied by (X plus .474266))

---

*Unless you are a math wiz, you won't want to deal with this formula (we don't). Instead, use our easy nose chill index:

FROZEN FOURSOME NOSE CHILL INDEX FORMULA

If drippage from your nose freezes at a 90° angle, you may suspend play immediately.

15. TREKKING RESTRICTIONS

Players may traverse the frozen course using snowmobiles or four-wheel all-terrain vehicles, but should make an effort to stay to the side of the fairway and follow any cart paths they can recall from summer play. Players may also be pulled by sled dog or anyone willing or foolish enough to agree to pull them around by sled (see **Caddies**).

Snowshoes and cross-country skis, though legally allowed, are frowned upon and generally considered showboating: cross-training is not a recognized component of Tundra Golf, and any player discovered to be playing Tundra Golf in order to exercise is usually subjected to ridicule by fellow Tundra Golfers. Cross-country skis also make playing hillside lies especially difficult.

16. TUNDRA ROLL

If the frozen tundra causes your ball to roll out of bounds, you may have a free drop placing the ball in play no closer to the hole.

If, however, the ball travels out of bounds through the air, you're on your own.

17. WINTER RULES

While the U.S.G.A. does not endorse "winter rules," they are strictly enforced under the rules of the T.G.A. Remember, Tundra Golf rules apply either when the ground is frozen (i.e. ball must bounce on green like it is concrete), when you can walk across water hazards,* or both. Therefore, the game is played during traditional "winter" months, thus forcing all the rules herein to fall under the heading "Winter Rules."

The following restriction applies:

• *Surname Restriction*

"Winter Rules" do not include rules concocted by any member of your foursome whose last name happens to be "Winter."

*Ice thickness may vary; test ice at your own risk.

TUNDRA GOLF'S FANTASY HOLE

The par 5, 675-yard number 14 at the Admiral Richard
E. Byrd Country Club near Antarctica's Mt. Vaughn
(Note: actual distance may vary depending on ice floe).

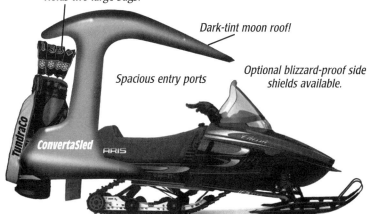

PART 3

TUNDRA GOLF
TIPS AND
TECHNIQUES

SANCTIONED TIPS FOR IMPROVING YOUR PLAY

The intricacies of Tundra Golf are vastly different from those of golf played in more moderate conditions. The cold and snow of tundra play affect players' club use, strategy, and, of course, skin dryness.

Golfers new to the tundra game should select a strong moisturizing lotion and try the tips on the following pages to help improve play.

Sanctioned Tip #1
Use an "Interlocking Grip"

When gripping your club, interlock the pinky of your lower hand with the index finger of your upper hand. This method keeps both fingers warmer, extending effective playing time.

Sanctioned Tip #2
Master the "Bump and Run"

Because frozen Tundra Golf greens can be as hard as concrete, chipped balls tend to roll well past the cup—lack of friction eliminates backspin. In other words, frozen greens don't hold. Chip with very little arc and aim well short of the cup. Remember: The only bite you'll get on tundra greens is frostbite.

Sanctioned Tip #3
Play the Drifts

Because of ball roll on frozen greens, you may wish to avoid reaching greens from fairway or tee shots, as balls tend to roll or even bounce well beyond your target. There's nothing like a nice, soft snow drift to bail out in before playing a biteless green. However, because locating balls becomes more difficult in deeper drifts, use this method only if you have plenty left in your bag.

❄ *A player may also gain added ball loft by utilizing the scoop of a solid drift. This is particularly useful when exiting a trap without a wedge.*

Sanctioned Tip #4
Know Your Ball Chill Index

Ball compression goes down as the temperature drops, reducing ball density. This can be either an advantage or a disadvantage to players: low compression can create unusually long shots, but it can also make club choice difficult (see *Maintain Ball Temperature*, on the next page). Because of this, liquid-center balls are not recommended—and can be highly dangerous—unless players maintain proper ball temperature. Try to use balls whose compression fits the temperature; follow the ball chill index below.

Temperature	Best Ball to Use
>33°F / >1°C	Not considered true Tundra Golf
23° to 32°F / -5° to 0°C	90 compression; any cover.
12° to 22°F / -12° to -6°C	80 compression; soft cover.
0° to 11°F / -18° to -11°C	Any (it really doesn't matter, they all play like rocks).
< 0°F / <-18°C	Go home to your loved ones.

Sanctioned Tip #5
Maintain Ball Temperature

In order to judge which club will provide you with the necessary distance, keep your ball in a glove or a warm jacket pocket or electric hunting socks (as allowed under Rule 2) to warm balls between shots.* Keeping the ball's temperature above 60° Fahrenheit will maintain proper compression, and balls will generally travel as far with the same club as they do during summer play.

Experienced Tundra Golfers may recall the ParPoacher,™ an ill-fated ball-warming product that was forced off the market due to misuse, despite its clear warning that it should be used for golf balls and golf balls alone!

*You could also utilize armpits and crotch pants pockets, but be careful: make sure you face partners and announce loudly when removing ball from crotch pocket to avoid being accused of "yellowing snow" to allow for a better lie.

NON-SANCTIONED TIPS FOR CREATING AN ADVANTAGE

Let's face it: if you're addicted to golf so much so that you choose to play Tundra Golf, you probably are also willing to go to great lengths to win. While the T.G.A. hardly endorses cheating, we do recognize that playing during the colder months does create certain tactical temptations that may not be easy to avoid. So that all of you new to Tundra Golf can start on equal footing, we have decided to grace the following pages with the five most popular methods used by T.G.A. members to "create advantages" for themselves.

Non-Sanctioned Tip #1
Icing the Putter

Pour liquid on an opponent's putter head just before he removes the club from his bag. The club head will freeze to the exposed skin of your opponent's hand, forcing him to walk about two holes with the putter under his armpit until he can remove his hand from the putter head without surgery.

Non-Sanctioned Tip #2
Pre-Cracked Pins

If your foursome is using sticks in place of flags to mark cups on greens (see rule #6a), volunteer to place the "pins" ahead of time and use prefractured sticks, so that even putters with the softest touch will break them, adding a stroke to their score (be careful, though: make sure you're "away" from the sabotaged greens).

Non-Sanctioned Tip #3
Horning an Opponent

When playing during deer hunting season, you may gain an advantage by placing a rack of deer antlers on your opponent's bag. It will be hard for him or her to concentrate after just one wayward hunter takes a few pot shots.

Non-Sanctioned Tip #4
Trick Balls

Replace your opponents' orange balls with gag balls that turn from orange to white during flight. They'll be buying balls and taking penalty strokes in no time (see rule #2c).

Non-Sanctioned Tip #5
The Cold Bath

Scout the course before your opponents arrive and remove all the "thin ice" signs from ponds and lakes.

The Frozen Foursome.

Dress like a TGA Pro with Official Tundra Golf Association apparel—available exclusively from the Bad Dog Boutique. 1/800-270-5863

High quality embroidered TGA logo golf caps, knit polos and our rugged two-color screened sweatshirts all make great gifts! Call to order today!

TOUR THE BAD DOG KENNEL

If you're enjoying this book, you'll also enjoy these other books from our kennel.

How to Get Rid of a Telemarketer
Rubber Chickens for the Soul
Who Packed Your Parachute?
The Habits of Seven Highly Annoying People

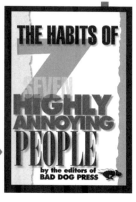

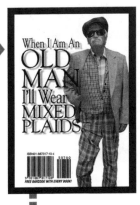

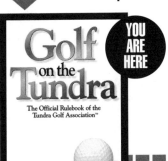

YOU
ARE
HERE

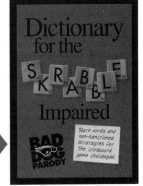

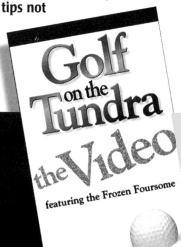